GW00401820

£7.99

we ❤ love you...

PUGS

A 2012 Annual

Compiled by David Clayton
Designed by Duncan Drummond

Contents

Why Own a Pug?

Welcome to the Pug Annual 2012 with everything you could ever want to know about these adorable little dogs. If you are a Pug owner, you'll already know what a delight it is to have one as a member of your family and what characters they are.

There are many reasons to own a Pug but the loyalty and affection they will give you for providing them with a loving home is probably the most rewarding. These little guys have so much love to give and they make wonderful family pets. They have great temperaments and love children – and children love them – though they do have their little, shall we say, habits?

Pugs are famous for passing gas often, so be prepared to have plenty of laughs – and pegs – after they've eaten because chances are, dinner will make an appearance as a stinky odour at some point! And Pugs can be stubborn, too! They may be small, but they have their own mind and if they want to do something – or don't – they will let you know. They are not demanding, don't

require around the clock entertainment and are happy with a quick walk round the block and some TLC every now and then. They snort, can be full of mischief and snore – but they will also become a big part of your family and maybe even take over if you allow it! They love nothing more than to be with their owners and will sleep at your feet, curl up next to you on the couch and sleep under your bed if they're allowed to. If you've already got a Pug, you'll know all the above to be true – if you haven't got one yet but are going to get one, you'll soon find out for yourself. This is a little dog with a BIG personality!

Looking After Your Pug

Some dogs need lots of love, care and attention and while that is true for Pugs, they don't need constant babysitting!

Your Pug is a lively and intelligent dog, but he doesn't require ten walks a day and a swim across a lake! One good walk a day will keep him fairly happy, but it goes without saying that he will enjoy two or three given the chance, so the more he has, the happier he'll be!

One thing these little fellas don't like is heat, so if it's hot and sunny, find a nice shady spot for your Pug and let him take it nice and easy. The reason is that Pugs are brachycephalic – this means they have a narrowed airway. If he gets hot, he won't be able to cool himself down by panting like other dogs so remember: heat + Pugs = bad!

Another important thing to think about is weight – you can't let your Pug get fat because his health will suffer, he will develop breathing problems and he may become ill. No matter how much you love him and want to give him special treats, you have to think about his well-being, so stick to his daily meals with the odd special (and small) treat for when he's been really good.

Pugs have very short, smooth coats so brush him regularly with a firm bristle dog brush and give him a shampoo every now and then, but apart from that, this is all the grooming he needs.

One thing to remember – dry him as quickly as possible so he doesn't catch a chill – like heat and weight problems, this could affect his breathing.

Now we all know what a handsome dog Pugs are – that's why you've got one, right? Well, those little folds in his skin need to be cleaned at least once a week but two or three times a week if possible.

No air circulates underneath the folds and this is where harmful bacteria could gather and cause infection. It's a simple job and cotton buds or clean tissues will do the job perfectly.

Follow the above advice and you'll have a happy, healthy Pug! There are plenty of books on Pugs available in good pet shops, libraries and the internet, so if in doubt, check it out!

Pug Puppies - Aren't They Cute?!

Pug pups are especially sweet. They are like little plush toys and once you look deep into those big eyes, you are smitten for life! Scattered around the cute pups below are some useful facts and advice...

Fact: It's always advisable to get your puppy from a reputable Pug breeder as a good, strong bloodline will reduce the risk of health problems.

Fact: Start training your puppy as soon as possible – they can be stubborn and have a mind of their own so be patient – they will get there eventually but they may enjoy pup status for up to TWO years!

Fact: When starting obedience training, be firm, confident and gentle and have a treat ready as reward-based instructions tend to get better results!

Fact: Pug puppy potty training can take time – stick to a routine and again, have plenty of patience. There will be accidents from time to time because they have small bladders, but everything will eventually click into place.

Fact: Pug pups love to chew and will eat anything, so make sure they have a favourite chewy toy to play with from day one – this will save them eating shoes and furniture and other household items which could do them harm and annoy you in the process.

Fact: Pups need a healthy, balanced diet with fresh water each day – get advice from vets or breeders before deciding which food to buy.

Fact: Pugs can't afford to get too hot or too cold so make sure they have a nice cool spot to lie in while you're out of the house. Keep them out of hot sun and in the winter, buy a little body warmer jacket to keep them snug.

Fact: Get your pup a nice collar with his name, your phone number and address on just in case he ever gets lost.

Fact: Depending on where you go and who you buy from, your pup could cost you anywhere from £300 to £1500.

Fact: Pups need grooming with a firm brush regularly. Get into good habits early on by cleaning under the folds of their skin at least once a week and check their eyes, ears and clip their claws at least once every month.

Reader's Story: Wilson

By Laura Lemmon, West Midlands

Pugs have always caused a debate...are they cute or are they ugly? I like to think of them as unique looking and, I'm sorry, but who could possibly resist those huge brown eyes?

After much nagging on my part, Wilson arrived in our lives at four months old - he was a bag of saggy skin but with amazing huge eyes which, in the early years, very much expressed "forgive me" rather than "spoil me". I soon realised why. I have mourned the loss of two fabulous pairs of shoes and many, many slippers! He still manages to catch me out to this day and loves when I am about to hang out the washing, I can see him willing me to drop a sock!

But, despite this, he learned discipline fast and didn't require any puppy training classes. Pugs are intelligent and very responsive to your tone of voice, he soon learned compliments from scoldings!

Wilson likes to strut rather than walk, he likes fuss and attention, and knows he'll get it. When we're out and about, we get stopped by people all the time wanting to fuss him. Wilson likes the ladies too but this has caught him out and he has actually walked into many lampposts and hedges checking out the ladies! Honestly! And yes, patio doors have caused him confusion too! I think this is where Pugs get their flat faces from!

Wilson's favourite thing to do is just cuddle - he'll watch me from a distance as I go about the daily household tasks and when he sees me going into the lounge he knows it's cuddle time, he'll even nudge my arm into position so he can cuddle right into my waist - we're talking proper cuddles here!

Five years on and Wilson definitely gets more Christmas presents than us, he is so much more than man's best friend, he is very much a family member in our house. I can't remember what life was like before him - it must have been very dull!

Wordsearch

Can you find the 10 things related to Pugs – or dogs in general - in the Wordsearch below? Remember, the words can be up, down, diagonal or horizontal.

BALL
BASKET
BISCUIT
BONE
COLLAR
LEAD
STICK
TAIL
TREATS
WALKIES

T	L	K	V	N	R	S	R	B
K	C	I	T	S	E	D	A	T
B	T	F	H	I	W	S	L	I
F	Z	L	K	V	K	R	L	U
Q	L	L	I	E	H	B	O	C
V	A	E	T	A	E	A	C	S
W	L	H	A	N	T	L	N	I
P	V	F	O	D	N	L	M	B
K	M	B	T	R	E	A	T	S

Answers on p60

Spot the Difference

Use your acute detective skills to spot the 10 differences between the two pictures below.

Pugalicious!

Feeding your Pug – dos and don'ts

Forget chocolate and marrow bones – your Pug may want to eat the things other dogs eat, but they won't do him any good. Here are some tips to help keep your little fella healthy and happy...

1 Don't let your Pug eat whenever they want – these little guys will eat all day if you let them, so get into a routine and stick to it. Try three moderate feeds per day – morning, lunchtime and evening depending on their age (see chart below). A third of a cup of high quality dried feed should be more than enough, but check with your local vet if you're unsure.

2 If you work or are at school it is wise to keep the drinks

to some kind of schedule so there are no accidents! Try water with each feed and then as much they need when you get home – plus more if it's hot.

3 Pugs like to gulp their food, so if you ever do give them a recommended treat, make sure it's a bite-sized piece so they don't choke on something bigger.

4 Stewed chicken and brown rice is an excellent meal for any Pug. Use dark meat only; chicken legs are a great choice. Stew the legs until the meat can be easily separated. Let the mixture cool until the meat can be safely handled. Remove the meat from the

20

bone and strain the liquid through a cheesecloth strainer to remove all fat and gristle. Return the liquid to the pot and add enough water to cook the rice. Cut the chicken into Pug-sized pieces while the rice is cooking. When the rice is ready, add the meat and it's dinnertime! You can make extra and freeze for another day.

5 Scrambled eggs and vegetables are a great way to get your Pug off to an energetic start. If you're using two eggs, remove one yolk and scramble the rest in a pan with low fat milk. Mix in some diced green beans and a bit of shredded reduced fat cheese. Let cool and serve.

6 NEVER feed your Pug chocolate – it could kill them. Chocolate contains caffeine and theobromine, two ingredients that stimulate the central nervous and cardiovascular systems. The amounts of these ingredients won't adversely affect humans but can cause serious side effects and even death in Pugs since they're considerably smaller than humans. If your Pug somehow gets hold of chocolate, take the dog to your vet and bring any remaining chocolate with you to help the vet diagnose the severity of the situation. Different types of chocolate contain varying amounts of caffeine and theobromine with unsweetened or baking chocolate being the worst culprit.

7 Another reason never to give your Pug a human treat is the possibility it will include Xylitol - an all-natural sweetener that's found mostly in desserts, sweets, cookies, cupcakes and gum made especially for people with diabetes. More and more sugar-free products are starting to

use Xylitol so if you own a Pug, be careful because after eating just a small amount, a dog's blood-sugar levels drop. The dog will next become lethargic, possibly start vomiting, and likely will have trouble standing. Lesions, internal bleeding and liver failure have also been reported. Please feed your Pug with the greatest of care and watch out, because they will eat anything given the opportunity.

8 Always keep table scraps and general waste out of your Pug's reach because high fat foods can lead to a serious condition called pancreatitis. Symptoms of pancreatitis appear quickly and include severe pain in the abdomen, vomiting, and sometimes diarrhoea. If your Pug eats high fat foods and exhibits any of these symptoms, it needs medical attention - and fast.

Age	Times Per Day Amount Each Time
Puppy (3 to 6 months)	3 x ⅓ cup
Adolescent (6 months to 1 year)	2 x ¾ cup
Active Adult (1 to 8 years)	2 x ½ cup
Senior (8 years+)	2 x ⅓ cup

Hollywood Pugs!

Yes, Pugs are natural-born actors and love the camera. Here is the proof, with 12 Hollywood movies featuring our four-legged friends...

Hotel for Dogs

Yes, this is a movie any Pug would be proud to be in – only there are two in this picture – Frick and Frack!

Pug rating: 4 pugs

Heavenly Creatures

This movie stars a 17 year old Kate Winslet and the scene with the Pug is brief. Her on-screen sister gets a Pug puppy for Christmas. Although there are strong performances from the two girls, and quite a powerful movie on the nature of adolescent fantasy creation, it is not a film for everyone's taste.

Pug rating: 2 pugs

Cats and Dogs

You'd be disappointed not to find a Pug in this film – don't worry – there is!

Pug rating: 4 pugs

Disney's Pocahontas

Featuring a pampered Pug called Percy, this is the only animated Pug we've come across!

Pug rating: 2 pugs

102 Dalmatians

Glenn Close plays Cruella de Vil and gets upstaged by a Pug at dinner.

Pug rating: 3 pugs

Eloise at Christmastime, Eloise at the Plaza

Stanley and Jezebel star in this heart-warming tale. They both shared in playing the part of Eloise's pug, Weenie!

Pug rating: 3 pugs

Walk With Destiny

The Pug, Goodchance My Delila appeared in this movie alongside Sir Richard Burton who played Winston Churchill. Burton was so enamoured that he offered a large sum of money to buy her but the owner, Ellen Brown, declined.

Pug rating: 2 pugs

The Adventures of Milo and Otis

The greatest Pug movie ever? Originally released in 1986 in Japan, the original Japanese version ran for 90 minutes while the English version only goes on for 76 minutes. The English version includes a narration by Dudley Moore.

Pug rating: 4 pugs

Dune

A sci-fi movie that played to mixed reviews, but it does have a Pug appearance in it, so it can't be all that bad!

Pug rating: 1 pug

Men In Black

Even though Mushu, who played Frank the Pug, only has a small part, he steals the show, winning fans all over the world.

Pug rating: 5 pugs

MIB II

Mushu, the canine actor who played Frank the Pug, returns for Men in Black II with a much bigger part. A little bit of pug trivia: Mushu was seven years old when he did the sequel and so had a little grey fur which had to be covered by the make-up department!

Pug rating: 5 pugs

The Truth About Charlie

Starring Mark Wahlberg, the Pug in this film is seen being held by its owner in Paris with the river Seine in the background.

Pug rating: 1 pug

Re-tail Therapy

There is a vast range of plush outfits for your fashion-conscious pug to be seen in this season. Here are our favourite sets and accessories:

Monte Carlo Pet Carrier
£49.95

This stunning bag is ideal for those who want to make a statement! Its sleek curves and colour make it a very stylish, yet very practical pet carrier. Unlike ordinary bags, the Monte Carlo Pet Carrier is specifically designed to be a pet carrier, and can be used in several ways to make your Pug's journey as comfortable and as safe as possible. There is a fine mesh window that provides ventilation and makes it possible for your Pug to take in the view during your outing. The bag also has two different outer panels that can be zipped open for easy access. The interior is lined with animal print material and has a removable carpet for easy cleaning and a lead hook for extra safety. Plus, there is a little pocket for treats and credit cards!

Black leather diamante collar and lead set

£18.95

Sparkling Bling Collar & Lead Set. This black leather collar with stitched edging has a crystal encrusted buckle with three large bling sparkling diamante bones and a large sparkling diamante charm completes the look. Truly a glamorous addition to the wardrobe of any trendy Pug. Matching lead has a silver clip finished with another large sparkling diamante bone.

Cream/Pink Quilted & Hooded Bodywarmer
£22.95

Practical with a splash of bling! A cream hooded bodywarmer, trimmed with fuchsia pink piping and a diamante style belt loop. It also has a pocket and some shoulder detailing for visual impact. The soft fleece lining will certainly keep your Pug snug and warm, while the pop buttons fastening on the underbelly makes it easy to take on and off.

Miss Hollywood Supersoft Mink Coat
£26.95

This supersoft mink-style fur coat has got to be the height of luxury, fit for any Hollywood Diva! Made to the highest standards and beautifully lined it is guaranteed to keep her warm and looking glamorous, you can almost see the pair of you hitting that red carpet.

Grey Puffa Ski Parka

£23.95

A gorgeous grey puffa ski parka. The arms and hem are elasticised to ensure the best possible fit. The velcro fastening makes it easy to take on and off. The soft grey fleece lining will keep your pup cosy and warm.

Luxury Quilted Parka with Detachable Hood

£24.95

This is a luxuriously quilted Parka coat with a faux-fur trimmed detachable hood. It gives your Pug two styles in one: wear it as a parka or, when the hood is removed, it can be worn as a coat. The arms and hem are elasticised for a great fit. It fastens from the underside with three pop-on, pop-off chrome buttons and the inside is lined with a light brown fleece material. There are two pockets on the back which can be opened and closed with two zips.

Luxury Black/White Duffle Coat with Detachable Hood

£24.95

This tartan coat is cosy yet versatile. It can be worn with the faux-fur trimmed hood, to keep your pug snug or, remove the hood and wear it as a duffle coat. The elasticised arm and hem, alongside the velcro fastening, make for a great fitting coat. The soft black fleece lining will keep your Pug toasty warm. Perfect for the chillier weather!

Pampered Boy Luxury Gift Box Set

£58.95

A perfect gift for that spoilt little boy - a professionally gift-wrapped, luxurious Gift Box Set features a preferred collection of "Dashing in Blue" clothing...

- Blue & White Luxury Parka

- Blue Argyle Sweater

- 100% Cotton Blue Hoodie with vintage-look "Rock Star" design

- Blue Harness-Lined "Security On Patrol" T-Shirt

- Blue Leather Diamante "Kiss" Collar & Matching Blue Lead

An equivalent is available in pink for your little girl Pug.

Pug Poems

We scoured the world looking for the best Pug poems around – and here are four of the best.

A Pug is a Dog

by Kenn Nesbitt

A pug is a dog,
With a curlicue tail.
He eats like a hog,
And he snores like a whale.
He's flat in the snout,
And his belly is big.
The pug came about
Just by misspelling... pig.

What is the matter?

By Winston Churchill

Oh, what is the matter with poor
Puggy-Wug?
Pet him and kiss him and give him
a hug.
Run and fetch him a suitable drug.
Wrap him up tenderly all in a rug.
That is the way to cure Puggy-Wug.

Puggy Paws

by Chylo

What makes a pug so sweet?
Maybe it's those adorable feet;
The way they run around the house,
Or lay feet up on the couch.
Maybe it's those big round eyes?
Or the way they make your mood rise.
The funny way they run,
Or maybe because they're always fun!
All those cute little snores,
Or the fact that she never bores?
Those corkscrew tails,
Their sense of humour, it never fails.
Maybe just maybe, it's all the puggy paws
they leave in your heart!

Heart stealer

by Leanne Thomas

The day my pug arrived, just a puppy –
so cute!
I couldn't stop smiling – I just thought,
'You beaut!'
Her character shone through straight
from day one,
And I knew that together, we'd
have so much fun.
I bought her a basket, to rest
her sweet head,
I needn't have bothered, she made
straight for my bed!
To have such a little dog, create such
a snore,
Meant I had no option, but to
show her the door.
Don't worry, she is still with
me today and always will be,
My Pug stole my heart – as I'm sure you
can see!

Spot the Difference

Use your acute detective skills to spot the 10 differences between the two pictures below.

Pug Quiz

Test your knowledge on the little rascals!

1) True or false: Pugs don't like heat.

2) What is the average lifespan of a Pug? A) 5 B) 12 C) 16

3) Pugs are known as what type of dog? A) Game B) Microscopic C) Toy

4) True or false: Justin Bieber has three Pug dogs named Maple, Leaf and Syrup

5) A Pug's tail is what? A) Curly B) Floppy C) He doesn't have one

6) Which country are Pugs believed to originate from? A) China B) England C) Holland

7) True or false: Some Pugs can grow to three feet high and are known as 'Giant' Pugs.

8) What is a Pug's bark like? A) Loud B) They can't bark C) Very quiet

9) Which of these are Pugs NOT famous for: A) Breaking wind B) Snoring C) Burping

10) Which breed are Pugs distant relatives of? A) Dobermans B) Pekingese C) Yorkshire Terriers

Answers on p60

Pugword Puzzle

Can you solve our doggy crossword below? It's got plenty of Pug questions in, but some about other types of dog, too. Fill in the blanks by answering the questions below that match up to the number on the crossword – good luck!

DOWN

1 All dogs love to hear this word! (7)
3 You might shout this to your dog if you throw a stick (5)
4 You can buy very pretty ones for your Pug and they are useful for putting their names on (6)
6 Major competition top dogs enter every year (6)
7 You'll need this if you take your Pug out to the park (4)
8 Name of the Pug who starred in Men In Black (5)
9 They need these clipping regularly! (5)
10 They drink out of this (4)
12 A word that describes a Pug when he is being awkward! (8)
17 Your Pug does this when he is asleep (5)

ACROSS

2 Noise your dog makes when the postman calls (4)
4 Country Pugs are thought to originate from (5)
5 Pugs like to wear these in the winter (6)
10 People who specialise in dog care and selling puppies are called… (8)
11 Another name for a Pug puppy (6)
13 One of the first things a dog learns to do (3,4)
14 No dogs like going here! (4)
15 All Pugs have these! (3,4)
16 Your Pug loves these! (6)
18 Somewhere your dog might like to sleep (6)

Famous Pug Owners!

Here are some famous stars who own Pugs – or vice-versa!

Who?	Profession	Name
Balthazar Getty	Actor	Ajax and Daisy
Billy Joel	Singer	Sabrina
Rebecca Loos	Presenter	Bubu
Dennis Quaid	Actor	Pudgy
Jessica Alba	Singer	Sid and Nancy

Who?	Profession	Name
Jonathan Ross	TV presenter	Mr Pickles
Kelly Osbourne	Celebrity	Prudence
Mickey Rourke	Actor	Raphael
Gerard Butler	Actor	Lolita
Paula Abdul	Singer	Puggy Sue
Rick Springfield	Singer	Pearl
Nicola Roberts	Singer	Ronnie and Reggie
Rob Zombie	Movie director	Dracula
Ted Danson	Actor	Roxy
Kelly Brook	TV presenter	Rocky
Paris Hilton	Socialite	Mugsy

Pug Health Concerns

Loving your Pug means giving them the best possible care. Being aware of health problems that could occur could save their life one day. Hopefully, your Pug will live a long and happy life, but here are some things to watch out for...

Health problems in Pugs are usually related to their eyes, face and legs, even though other problems might exist. Please remember that every dog is different and that this is only a list of some of the most common health problems Pugs might experience. And as always, if your Pug is experiencing any kind of health problem, contact your vet immediately and get expert advice.

Leg and Knee Problems

Hip Dysplasia (HD):

Hip Dysplasia can be described as a bad fit between the two bones of the hip joint and is caused by malformation of one or the other. HD often causes stiffness in the hind legs, substantial pain and in more severe cases, lameness.

Patellar Luxation:

Patellar Luxation or kneecap dislocation occurs when the kneecap slides out of its groove. A Pug with Patellar Luxation can sometimes limp or walk on three legs. Surgery is often the treatment of choice here, since it is a serious health condition.

Eyes

Dry Eye Syndrome:

Dry Eye Syndrome is a quite common and potentially blinding condition, which develops due to the decline of tear production in the eye. Treatment consists of drug therapy and surgery.

Bilateral Cataracts:

Bilateral Cataracts are recognised by dense spots on the lens of the eye. These spots may cause partial or total loss of vision. In some cases surgery may help.

Entropion:

Entropion is a problem caused by the Pug's eyelashes irritating the surface of the eyeball. This should be treated since it might lead to more serious problems.

Progressive Retinal Atrophy (PRA):

PRA is the deterioration of the vessels around the retina. This condition usually begins with night blindness in younger dogs, but as their vision deteriorates it can lead to blindness. Since Pugs have such a short nose and such bulky eyes, they can easily scratch their corneas or even puncture their eyeballs. Therefore, though they are curious critters, try to keep them away from sharp objects at all times!

Breathing Problems

Tracheal Collapse:

Tracheal Collapse is a narrowing of the windpipe. Symptoms include a cough (especially after exercise) harsh breathing and gagging. Treatment consists of conservative therapy or surgery.

Elongated Soft Palate (ESP):

ESP is the obstruction of the dog's airways. Excessive gasping for air and the blocking of the Pug's vocal box are some of the signs. ESP can be corrected with surgery.

Stenotic Nares:

Stenotic Nares is a birth defect where the nostrils are too small and the Pug puppy has difficulties breathing through his nose. This condition puts a strain on the Pug's entire body and can lead to an enlargement of the heart, tracheal collapse and chronic bronchitis.

Pug Dog Encephalitis:

Pug Dog Encephalitis or PDE is an inflammatory disease of the brain that often causes seizures. If your Pug is experiencing seizures, he or she should definitely be tested for this disorder.

Demodectic Mange:

Lots of Pugs get Demodectic Mange, a parasitic skin disease caused by a mite which can cause hair loss and irritation. Demodectic Mange does require veterinary treatment, but it is usually easily cured with a shot and ointment.

Portosystemic Shunt (PSS):

A PSS is an abnormal vessel that allows blood to bypass the liver. As a result, the blood is not cleansed properly. Symptoms may include, but are not limited to, vomiting, diarrhoea, loss of appetite, hunger for non-food substances, depression and intolerance of protein-rich food.

Other common health problems include: heat stroke, skin allergies, obesity, arthritis, back problems and heart disease.

All the above may look worrying, but just remember - regular health checks at the vet's, a good diet and plenty of exercise will help keep your Pug happy and healthy for many years to come.

Pug Sketches

There are many ways to sketch a Pug and there are plenty of excellent examples around – here are some of the best, but on the page opposite, why not try sketching your own Pug and colouring him/her in?

Woof
down brownies

Pugs need high energy, low fat treats to keep healthy – try this recipe to make them the perfect reward – if you're a youngster, make sure a grown-up helps you with this!

1¼ pounds beef or chicken liver

2 whole eggs

3 tablespoons peanut butter

2 tablespoons whole wheat flour

1 cup cooked barley

2 cups wheat germ

1 tablespoon olive oil

Directions:

Pre-heat oven to 350 degrees F.

Grease a 9″ x 9″ baking dish.

Place liver in a blender and liquefy. Add eggs and peanut butter; blend until mixture is smooth.

In a bowl combine whole wheat flour, cooked barley and wheat germ. To this add liver mixture and olive oil; mix well. Spread into a greased baking dish and bake for 20 minutes.

When brownies are cool, cut into large or small squares, depending on the size of your dog. Place cooled brownies in airtight container and store in refrigerator.

Recipe will make: 1 to 2 dozen depending on how you cut them.

Before feeding your pug any foods that have different ingredients than they are used to, check with your local vet to make sure your pug is not allergic to any of the ingredients!

The **A-Z** of **Pugs**

A complete alphabet of Pug-related stuff!

A is for affectionate – as all Pugs are.

B is for bones – a dog's best friend!

C is for cats – Pugs largely get on with cats, mostly because they are around the same size!

D is for diet – Pugs need a balanced, healthy eating schedule.

E is for energetic – well, some Pugs are!

F is for family – Pugs are born to be family dogs.

G is for grooming - which all Pugs need doing regularly.

H is for happy – Pugs are happiest when they are with their owners.

I is for independence – Pugs have a mind of their own!

J is jacket – Pugs need keeping warm on their winter walks.

K is for kids – Pugs adore children and children love them.

L is for lead – a quick shake of it and your Pug will know he's off for a walk.

M is for master – a Pug's best friend!

N is for naughty – Pugs have a mischievous nature and enjoy doing things they aren't supposed to.

O is for overweight – a dangerous thing for Pugs to be.

P is for Puglet – a Pug puppy.

Q is for Queen Victoria – who once owned a Pug!

R is for rescue – there are several organisations that specialise in finding rescued Pugs new homes.

S is for stubborn – as most Pugs are!

T is for Toy – the category of dog Pugs come under.

U is for upset – your Pug will be upset if he is regularly left alone.

V is for vaccine – Pugs need their injections because they can pick up infections.

W is for wind – and not the sort that blows through the trees!

X is for x-ray – Pugs can develop health problems where x-rays might be needed to clarify issues.

Y is for yelp – Pugs may be small but their bark really is worse than their bite!

Z is for Zzzzzz – you'll know when your Pug is asleep because chances are he'll snore!

The Pug Dog Welfare & Rescue Association

Registered Charity No. 276067

I f the ladies who originally formed Pug Welfare in 1973 could look on now, they would hardly believe their eyes. The Pug has grown in popularity over the last 10 years and is now one of the world's most popular dogs. Those of us who love them unconditionally can sort of understand this, but we all find it hard to believe the commercial breeding and puppy farms that have taken the dog from being rarely seen, to, as has happened recently, 13 dogs needing homes in as many days.

Over the years we have had a bitch in whelp, a five week old puppy and old, really sick dogs who have no quality of life but whose owners cannot cope with making a final decision. It is so sad.

We regularly have Pugs that need homes because of relationship break ups, owners moving and unable to take them with them and all the other reasons that make owning a dog no longer possible.

Occasionally we have had Pugs that have been kept in sheds, abandoned in shopping centres or just generally lost because they have been turned out. But usually it is the rather sad change of circumstances that find us taking a Pug to a new home that is as far as possible matched like-for-like. If the Pug comes from a home where there are children it makes sense for them to go to a similar home, or if it has lived a quiet life we would find a similar home. You can see from the picture below that young Thomas and Billy are the best of friends.

Sometimes a Pug arrives in a very bad state and will stay with a member of Welfare to be nursed back to health and then re-homed. Sometimes they arrive absolutely filthy with damaged eyes or with skin conditions, nails growing into their pads and deaf because their ears are blocked with debris. We are rewarded as they recover and learn to trust the humans who are doing their best to help them.

One of the saddest stories I have heard was of the now 14½ year old bitch, Alice, who was found in a bath with her remaining puppy, Reuben. It was thought that Alice had eaten the remains of her other puppies to stay alive. The bitch was 10 years old when she had the litter and the lady who worked at the vet's and who now so proudly owns her, took her and

50

the puppy on. They are pictured (below right), happy, healthy and absolutely adored.

We have a great system for getting our dogs from A to B. If a Trustee is geographically unable to collect the Pug, we have our Friends of Pug Welfare. These wonderful people will, if necessary, abandon everything and get in their cars and go straightaway to collect the dog in need. Just occasionally it really is like that, but we normally have a little more time in which to organise collection and re-homing.

Veterinary expenses increase every year and we fund raise to cover these costs. In 2010 we spent £4,599 which was light in comparison with the previous year's fees of £7,572. To cover these expenses we have great fun with our Pug Parties which are held at two or three venues each year.

The main Party is at Crowhurst in Surrey which is really the birthplace of Welfare and where it started all those years ago and it has been held every second Sunday in July for as long as I can remember. We play games, we have fancy dress,

the Welfare Parade and an excellent tea. Pug parties are a great way to make friends with other like minded people and pictured below are some of our Welfare dogs attending our most recent fundraiser.

We have a website which will keep you up-to-date with what is going on and a webshop where you can buy the sort of Puggy things that you cannot get anywhere else. Do visit us there or become a Friend by making a donation of not less than £10 a year. When you join, you receive a badge, a car sticker and a newsletter twice a year.

For more information, contact:
Wendy Tudor-Morgan
63 Berwick Rd, Little Sutton,
Cheshire CH66 4PW
0151 347 1717

www.pugwelfare-rescue.org.uk

Pugs on the Net

You can swap stories, seek advice and read about everything you need to know about Pugs on the internet. Here are 10 sites we love – but remember, check first it's OK before going on-line....

Pug Center
http://www.pugcenter.com/ - a website set up for Pug lovers, by Pug lovers. Great, informative and easy to use.

Pugs.co.uk
http://www.pugs.co.uk/ - a UK site, well presented with excellent information and advice.

Pugs.com
http://www.pugs.com/ - honest and interesting, this is another terrific site. Well worth a visit.

Pug World
http://www.pugworld.co.uk/ - a forum for Pug owners to exchange stories and advice.

Pugs UK Unlimited
http://www.animates.co.uk/pugsuk/ - basic but interesting site.

Pugs.nl
http://www.pugs.nl/ - Pugs have always been popular in Holland and this Dutch site – in English – proves the point.

Dog breed info
http://www.dogbreedinfo.com/pug.htm - not a specialised Pug site but useful nonetheless.

Pug Village
http://www.pugvillage.com/ - this site claims to be the most popular Pug website in the world. It's good and definitely worth a look.

Pwll Clai Pugs
http://www.pwllclaipugs.com/web/splash.php - a site that doesn't blow its own trumpet, but there's loads of info and advice on here. A must for anyone owning or thinking of owning a Pug.

Wikipedia's Pug Pages
http://en.wikipedia.org/wiki/Pug - as you'd expect, a one-stop shop for everything you could ever want to know about Pugs and their history.

Pugs:
Did You Know?

Think you know all there is to know about Pugs? Read on and see if you actually do!

- Pugs originate from Tibet, high up in the Andes mountain range.

- Pugs are one of the oldest recorded breeds in history and the earliest known mention of them is from almost 2,500 years ago in ancient China.

- Pugs are famous for breaking wind! It's just the way they're built! They snore a lot, too!

- The name 'Pug' didn't come about until sometime in the 1700s when, it is believed, the 'Pug Dog' received his name due to the similarity between the facial expression of our furry friends and the facial expressions of the marmoset or 'Pug Monkey', another popular pet at that time.

- The Pug's closest relative is the Pekingese – a distant cousin who seems to have many similarities to the Pug bloodline.

- Pugs have several other names they are or have been known as, including 'Chinese pug', 'Dutch bulldog', 'Dutch mastiff' and 'Mini mastiff'.

- Many trees, plants and shrubs can cause serious health issues to development if your Pug eats them. Asparagus ferns, pothos, poinsettia, amaryllis, Boston ivy, tulip and narcissus bulbs, lilies, azalea, rhododendron, oleander, cyclamen, yew and kalanchoe are just a few of the many potential hazards, so if you see them about to eat any plants – inside or outside the home – stop them immediately.

- Pugs come in several colours: fawn, apricot fawn, silver or black. There is also the rarer white pug which gets its coat via breeding or albinism. A silver coat is characterised by a very light coloured coat, and absence of black guard hairs.

- Queen Victoria, Winston Churchill and William of Orange all owned Pugs.

- It is thought the first Pugs appeared in England in 1860 when soldiers returning from battles in China brought the breed back with them.

- The average weight of a Pug is between 14 and 18 pounds and the average life expectancy is somewhere between 10 and 12 years.

- A Pug is part of a category of dogs known as 'Toy' because of their sizc, weight and unique attributes.

- Like most dogs, Pugs do like to chew things - which can be a problem! This can be easily solved, however. If a Pug is given plenty of chewy toys, their attention will be devoted more to those toys and less towards other items. With enough firm training, however, these dogs will know what items are off limits to them and will grow into responsible pets.

Reader's Story: Pixie

By Judith Apter, London

What attracted me to the Puggle was a phrase out of a Puggle book that read: "If anything is out of place or the routine changes, the Puggle will immediately recognise the difference and may give you a look or a bark in protest."

This describes my personality to a tee! I love and adore routine and order and so I thought we would be a match made in Doggie Heaven and I have to say I have been well and truly puggled and, along with the rest of our family, am totally besotted !

Also, I read that one of the Puggle's most endearing qualities is that it desires to be in your company just as much as you do in its company. This is certainly true of Pixie, who became the most popular member of the family within hours of her arrival!

She makes sure she is at the heart of the family, enjoying rests on her furry beanbag in the kitchen.

Pixie is an adorable, sweet tempered, wrinkle-faced, loyal dog who never

growls at anybody or anything except her spiky, green ball!

She is loving and lovable and always ready for a cuddle but playful and lively too, loving her two walks every day. Recently, she found a dummy in the park. Who says Pixie isn't my little baby?

She loves going out for walks, especially when they involve a café or lunch in a dog-friendly pub/restaurant.

We always take her special water bottle

with us, in case she gets thirsty. She sleeps in her crate downstairs but

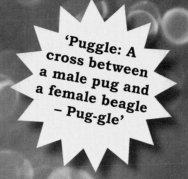

'Puggle: A cross between a male pug and a female beagle – Pug-gle'

there's nothing like her enthusiasm in the mornings when she comes bounding up the stairs to greet us, jumping on the bed and covering us in

doggy kisses and Pixie licks! Once this mission is accomplished, she snuggles down under the covers, sometimes with her head on the pillow, ready for her morning snooze.

It's not just triplets, Dan, Chloe and Livvy who go to school every morning; Pixie comes too! Strapped into her seatbelt, when the school bell chimes, and the kids rush out, she watches out of the window and cries as she says

goodbye to her brother and sisters.

Pixie has a very distinctive tail, curly like a Walnut Whip, always spinning round because she's such a happy dog.

Pixie has a hearty appetite and is not very picky about what she eats. In fact, she believes that more of anything is what she wants. Roast chicken and apple are her two favourite foods.

Pixie's Favourite Things

Shredding tissues

Playing chase and wrestling with other puppies

Sitting at the table and eating a sausage in the park café after a walk

Standing in the shower with the water dripping down on her, having a drink

Going in the car to school and being fussed over by all the children

Licking Adam's face clean

Sleeping on her beanbag

Cuddles, cuddles and cuddles!

Answers Page

Wordsearch solution: page 18

T	L	K	V	N	R	S	R	B
K	C	I	T	S	E	D	A	T
B	T	F	H	I	W	S	L	I
F	Z	L	K	V	K	R	L	U
Q	L	L	I	E	H	B	O	C
V	A	E	T	A	E	A	C	S
W	L	H	A	N	T	L	N	I
P	V	F	O	D	N	L	M	B
K	M	B	T	R	E	A	T	S

Pug Quiz solution: page 34

1) True
2) C - 12
3) C - Toy
4) False
5) A - Curly
6) A - China
7) False
8) A - Loud
9) C - Burping
10) B - Pekingese

Pugword Puzzle solution: page 35

Spot the Difference: page 19

Spot the Difference: page 31

Where's Pug?